The World of Horses

Grayscale Adult Coloring Book
by Ruth Sanderson

Colored by

_____

The World of Horses

These thirty-six images are original paintings of horses that I carefully converted to grayscale for your coloring enjoyment. I have been painting horses for over 40 years! I suggest colored pencils for best results coloring grayscale images on this paper. I like to use Prismacolor Premiers, though there are many other good brands. Some people use pastels for skies and white gel pen for highlights, as well as other media. Experiment! If you are new to grayscale, it is quite different from coloring line art, but you will soon get the knack and fall in love with grayscale coloring!

Horse coloring tips

Look for some color photos of horses to study all the different color possibilities. I suggest choosing at least four pencils from light to dark that would create a desired coat color. Suggestions for the cover image of a blood-red bay: Light Peach (PC927), Mineral Orange (PC1033) Pumpkin Orange (PC 1032), Chestnut (PC 1081). For a video demonstration of coloring this image, and other colored pencil demos, video visit my YouTube Channel:

https://www.youtube.com/user/ruthsander

I start with layers of the lightest (highlight) color first, overlapping the surrounding mid-tones, then work in layers of medium tone pencil over the entire horse, following the shading pattern in the grayscale and layering more color in darker areas. Add more layers with the next (slightly darker) tone, working it into darker areas, usually the undersides and contours away from the light source. I use the darkest color for outlining and carefully deepening shadow areas, etc. I suggest a Dark Brown or Sepia for eyes. I then go back in with the medium pencils, and the light pencil in lighter areas, to blend everything together, pressing a bit harder to burnish the colors together, and hitting the highlights again with the lightest pencil. For an even smoother finish try blending with Gamsol or a colorless marker, making sure you have enough layers of pigment on the paper. (Note: blending pencils do not work very well on grayscale, as they can sometimes bring the gray back up.) You can add even more layers and colors after you blend with the marker or Gamsol.

I invite you to join my RuthSandersonArt Coloring Group on Facebook—
I love to see how people color my images!

Happy Coloring,

Ruth

Sign up for my newsletter for coloring book news and free downloads: www.ruthsanderson.com

ABOUT THE ARTIST

Ruth's favorite stories growing up were horse stories and fairy tales. These subjects have always been her favorite things to draw and paint. Ruth has created many award-winning fairy tale picture books for children, and she has been illustrating the HORSE DIARIES chapter book series from Random House for many years. She also illustrated the first paperback editions of the BLACK STALLION series. New editions of her fairytales, including retellings of *The Golden Mare, the Firebird and the Magic Ring, Cinderella, The Twelve Dancing Princesses,* and *The Snow Princess,* can be ordered from any local bookstore, Amazon, or from Interlink Publishing: www.interlinkbooks.com.

Ruth has many other coloring books currently available on Amazon and from her ETSY shop in PDF form, and more books planned for the future, including at least one more horse coloring book as well as a Mother Goose book, another Christmas coloring book, and more books in the Beautiful Fairy Tales series.

Ruth teaches writing and illustrating in the summer MFA program at Hollins University in Roanoke, Virginia, and lives the rest of the year with her family in Massachusetts with assorted cats and her beloved Quarter Horse, Shadow.

Sign up for her newsletter at www.ruthsanderson.com
and find her on Facebook at ruthsandersonart

The World of Horses
Grayscale images Copyright © 2018 by Ruth Sanderson
All rights reserved.

Terms of Use:
In addition to coloring the pictures in this book you may photocopy these images on your paper of choice to color for your personal use, but you do not have permission to distribute or give away the uncolored images online.

GOLDEN WOOD STUDIO
PO Box 285
Easthampton, MA 01027
USA

ISBN-13:
978-1984037916

ISBN-10:
1984037919

Printed by Create Space

Happy Coloring!
Ruth and Shadow

Made in the USA
Middletown, DE
01 March 2019